Construction Mediation
From the Job Site to Resolution

CONSTRUCTION MEDIATION

First edition. March 10, 2026.

ISBN: 979-8233870941

Written by Nicholas Salerno III.

BY NICHOLAS SALERNO III

Contractor Protection Series
BOOK 1

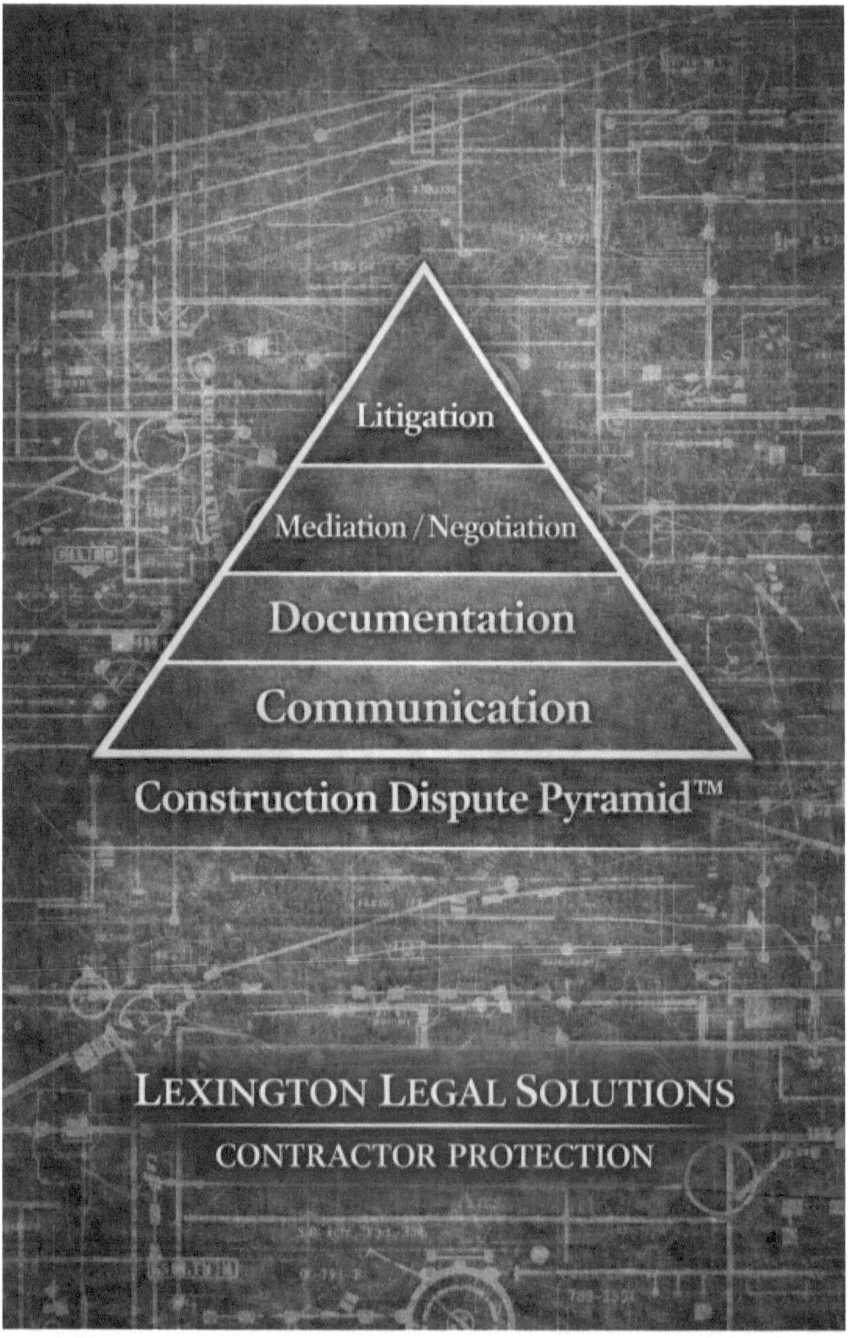
Litigation
Mediation / Negotiation
Documentation
Communication
Construction Dispute Pyramid™
LEXINGTON LEGAL SOLUTIONS
CONTRACTOR PROTECTION

Legal Disclaimer

This book is intended for educational and informational purposes only.

The material presented in this book reflects the professional experience, research, and personal observations of the author in the construction industry and dispute resolution field. It is designed to help contractors, subcontractors, and homeowners better understand common issues that arise during construction projects and how disputes are often addressed.

Nothing in this book should be interpreted as legal advice.

The author, Nicholas Salerno III, and Lexington Legal Solutions are not providing legal representation through this publication. Every construction project and legal situation is unique, and the laws governing construction disputes, contracts, licensing, mechanic's liens, and consumer protections vary by state and jurisdiction.

Readers should consult with a licensed attorney or qualified professional for legal advice specific to their situation.

While the author has made every effort to ensure the accuracy and usefulness of the information presented, no guarantees are made regarding the outcomes of any particular dispute, negotiation, or legal matter.

The strategies, frameworks, and examples provided in this book—including the Construction Dispute Pyramid™, Contractor Payment Triangle™, and Contractor Protection Framework™—are educational tools intended to help readers better understand the dynamics of construction projects and dispute resolution.

Use of the information contained in this book is at the reader's own discretion and risk.

By reading this book, the reader acknowledges that the author and publisher shall not be held liable for any loss, damages, or legal consequences arising from the application or interpretation of the material presented.

For educational resources and contractor dispute guidance, visit **LexingtonLegalSolutions.com**

Introduction

My Journey From the Job Site to Construction Dispute Resolution

Construction is one of the most honest professions in the world.

You build something real. Something people live in. Something families depend on every single day.

But if you spend enough time in construction, you will learn something that every contractor eventually discovers:

Construction projects don't just build houses — they also create conflict.

Misunderstandings happen.

Money becomes tight.

Expectations change.

Communication breaks down.

And before anyone realizes what happened, a small issue can turn into a serious dispute.

Over the past decade, I have lived through many sides of the construction industry.

I didn't start as a lawyer or a mediator.

I started the same way many contractors do — working with tools in my hands.

Early in my career I worked as an electrician, troubleshooting complex electrical systems in high-end homes. Electrical work teaches you something important: when something fails, you have to think like a detective. You follow the wires, test the circuits, and slowly work your way back to the source of the problem.

Later I worked as a handyman, doing whatever work I could find to support myself and build experience. I repaired homes, installed fixtures, and learned how to solve problems with very limited resources.

Like many small contractors, I hustled.

Eventually I began managing larger projects. At one point I coordinated crews replacing toilets across California in large commercial buildings. It wasn't glamorous work — in fact it was often dirty and exhausting — but it taught me how to manage crews, coordinate schedules, and deal with the unexpected challenges that show up on every job site.

Later I expanded into lighting retrofits and other construction projects.

Eventually I earned my contractor's license as a painting contractor and founded **Royal Painting**, a company that has now been serving homeowners for more than ten years.

Running a painting company might sound simple to some people, but anyone who has been in the construction business knows the truth:

You are not just painting houses.

You are managing crews.

You are dealing with schedules.

You are coordinating materials.

You are solving jobsite problems every day.

And perhaps most challenging of all...

You are working with people.

Homeowners often invest enormous emotional and financial energy into their homes. Many projects involve their life savings or loans they will spend years paying off. Naturally, expectations can be high.

At the same time, contractors operate in a demanding environment. Materials change. Schedules slip. Weather interferes. Subcontractors make mistakes. Payments get delayed.

In other words, the construction industry sits right at the intersection of **money, expectations, and stress.**

That combination is the perfect recipe for conflict.

Over the years I began to see patterns in how construction disputes happen.

The same types of arguments appear again and again.

A homeowner believes work should have been included in the contract.

A contractor believes the homeowner is requesting extra work.

Payments are delayed because expectations were not clearly documented.

Small communication issues slowly grow into larger disputes.

Eventually someone threatens legal action.

I started realizing that many of these conflicts could have been prevented if both sides understood a few simple principles about how construction disputes actually work.

At the same time, I began studying the legal side of construction more deeply.

I studied construction law, mediation, and dispute resolution. I spent thousands of hours learning how disputes are handled through the legal system and how mediation can help resolve conflicts before they escalate into lawsuits.

During this time I also had the opportunity to speak in front of regional management teams at **Home Depot** regarding paint systems and construction practices. I met with executives from **Behr Paint**, one of the largest paint manufacturers in the country.

Experiences like these gave me a broader view of the construction industry — from the jobsite level all the way up to large corporate systems.

But what fascinated me most was not the technical side of construction.

It was the **human side of construction disputes**.

Why do disagreements escalate?

Why do simple problems turn into lawsuits?

Why do contractors and homeowners often feel like enemies, even though both sides originally wanted the same thing — a successful project?

Over time I came to a realization:

Most construction disputes are not really about construction.

They are about **communication, documentation, and expectations.**

When those three things break down, problems grow quickly.

This book was written to help contractors, homeowners, and construction professionals understand how disputes develop and how they can be resolved.

The goal of this book is not to turn readers into lawyers.

Instead, it provides a **practical roadmap for understanding construction conflict and resolving it effectively.**

Inside these pages you will learn:

- why construction disputes are so common
- how small jobsite issues turn into major conflicts
- how mediation works in the construction industry
- how both contractors and homeowners can prepare for dispute resolution
- how many conflicts can be resolved without expensive litigation

This book is also part of a larger system called the **Construction Resolution Series**, which provides practical guidance for navigating the most common legal and financial challenges in the construction industry.

Each book focuses on a specific area:

Construction Mediation – From the Job Site to Resolution

Understanding how disputes arise and how they can be resolved.

The Construction Dispute Playbook

Understanding the legal rules that govern construction projects.

Mechanic's Liens Made Simple

How contractors protect their right to payment.

The Contractor Survival Guide

Practical strategies for running a safe and successful construction business.

Together, these books form a practical system designed to help contractors and homeowners avoid unnecessary conflict and protect themselves when disputes arise.

Because in construction, conflict is not a possibility.

It is a reality.

The question is not whether problems will occur.

The question is **how prepared you will be when they do.**

My goal is simple:

To help you understand the system, protect yourself, and resolve disputes the right way.

Let's begin.

Chapter 1

The Reality of Construction Disputes

If you spend enough time in the construction business, you eventually discover a truth that surprises many people outside the industry:

Construction disputes are not unusual. They are inevitable.

Every contractor has experienced it.

A project begins with excitement. The homeowner is enthusiastic. The contractor is confident. Plans are discussed, materials are chosen, and the work begins.

For a while, everything moves forward smoothly.

Then something small happens.

A color looks different on the wall than the homeowner expected.

A fixture arrives later than planned.

A change request is made that was never written down.

At first it seems minor.

But if the situation is not handled carefully, that small issue can slowly grow into something much larger.

The homeowner becomes frustrated.

The contractor feels unfairly criticized.

Communication becomes tense.

Before long, the project that began with excitement becomes a source of stress for everyone involved.

This pattern happens across the construction industry every day.

Understanding why this happens is the first step toward preventing it.

Construction Is Built on Pressure

Most construction projects exist under pressure from the very beginning.

Homeowners often invest large amounts of money into their homes. For many families, a renovation project represents years of savings or a significant loan.

Naturally, they want everything to be perfect.

At the same time, contractors operate under their own set of pressures.

Construction schedules are tight. Materials must arrive on time. Crews must be coordinated. Weather conditions can interrupt progress. And contractors must manage cash flow carefully in order to keep the business operating.

Even a small delay or misunderstanding can affect the entire project.

When these pressures combine, even minor problems can feel much larger than they actually are.

The Expectation Gap

One of the most common causes of construction disputes is something I call **the expectation gap**.

The expectation gap occurs when the homeowner and the contractor believe different things about what the project includes.

This might involve:

- the scope of the work
- the timeline for completion
- the quality or appearance of the finished product
- what happens if something changes during the project

Sometimes the gap is obvious.

For example, a homeowner may request additional work that was never included in the contract.

Other times the gap is subtle.

A homeowner might expect a certain level of finish that the contractor never promised. The contractor may believe the job is complete, while the homeowner still sees unfinished details.

Neither side is necessarily acting in bad faith.

They simply started the project with different expectations.

When those expectations are not clarified early, the disagreement slowly grows.

Construction Projects Are Emotional

Another factor that makes construction disputes unique is that **homes are deeply personal spaces.**

For a contractor, the project may be one job among many.

For the homeowner, it is their living environment, their financial investment, and sometimes even their dream home.

Every decision feels important.

Every mistake feels personal.

When something goes wrong, emotions can rise quickly.

A homeowner who feels ignored may become angry.

A contractor who feels accused may become defensive.

Once emotions enter the conversation, it becomes much harder to resolve the problem calmly.

This is one reason why clear communication and documentation are so important in construction projects.

They help remove emotion from the discussion and focus on the facts.

The Communication Breakdown

In many construction disputes, the real problem is not the construction work itself.

The real problem is communication.

A contractor may assume the homeowner understands the process.

A homeowner may assume the contractor understands their expectations.

But assumptions can be dangerous.

Without clear communication, both sides begin to fill in the missing information with their own interpretation.

The homeowner might think:

"Why hasn't the contractor finished this yet?"

The contractor might think:

"Why is the homeowner complaining about something that was never part of the contract?"

Neither side realizes that the other is operating with different information.

Eventually frustration builds.

Communication becomes shorter and more defensive.

At that point, the dispute is no longer about solving the problem.

It becomes about **who is right and who is wrong.**

Money Changes the Conversation

Another moment when disputes often appear is when payments become involved.

Construction projects typically involve several stages of payment:

- deposit
- progress payments
- final payment

When everything is going well, these payments move forward smoothly.

But if the project encounters delays, misunderstandings, or dissatisfaction, payment discussions can quickly become tense.

A homeowner might delay payment because they feel the work is incomplete.

A contractor might stop work because payment has not been received.

This creates a situation where both sides feel justified in their position.

The homeowner believes they are protecting themselves.

The contractor believes they are being denied payment for work already completed.

Without a clear plan for resolving the disagreement, the situation can escalate rapidly.

When Small Problems Become Big Problems

Most construction disputes do not begin as major conflicts.

They begin as small problems that were never addressed properly.

A missed phone call.

An unclear text message.

A change that was discussed but never written down.

These small gaps slowly accumulate.

Eventually both sides begin to feel frustrated.

The homeowner might start researching contractor complaints online.

The contractor might begin preparing documentation to defend their work.

At this stage, the relationship between contractor and homeowner has shifted.

The focus is no longer on completing the project together.

The focus becomes **protecting oneself from the other party.**

Once a project reaches this stage, resolving the dispute becomes much more difficult.

The Truth About Construction Disputes

After many years in the construction industry, one truth becomes clear:

Most disputes are not caused by bad people.

They are caused by **systems that were not designed to prevent conflict.**

Contracts are often too vague.

Documentation is incomplete.

Communication happens casually instead of professionally.

These gaps leave both contractors and homeowners vulnerable when disagreements arise.

But there is good news.

When contractors and homeowners understand how disputes develop, they can take steps to prevent them.

And when disputes do occur, there are effective ways to resolve them without destroying the relationship or resorting to expensive legal battles.

This book will explore those solutions.

In the next chapter, we will introduce a framework that helps explain how construction disputes escalate — and how they can be resolved before they reach the most destructive stages.

This framework is called **The Lexington Legal Solutions Construction Dispute Pyramid**.

Understanding this simple model can change the way you approach every construction conflict.

And in many cases, it can prevent a dispute from becoming a lawsuit.

Chapter 2

The Lexington Legal Solutions Construction Dispute Pyramid™

If you want to understand how construction disputes develop—and more importantly how they can be resolved—you need a simple way to visualize the process.

Over the years, working on construction projects and studying dispute resolution, I began to notice a pattern.

Almost every dispute followed the same path.

It started small.

Then it grew.

Then it escalated into something much more serious.

Eventually I began explaining this pattern to contractors and homeowners using a simple model that I now call:

The Lexington Legal Solutions Construction Dispute Pyramid™

This framework helps explain how construction conflicts evolve and why some disputes spiral into lawsuits while others are resolved quickly and professionally.

Understanding this pyramid can help both contractors and homeowners keep problems at the lowest and most manageable level.

The Three Levels of the Dispute Pyramid

The Construction Dispute Pyramid has three levels.

From bottom to top they are:

Level 1 – Communication & Documentation

Level 2 – Mediation & Negotiation

Level 3 – Litigation

Most disputes should be resolved at the bottom of the pyramid.

Unfortunately, when problems are ignored or handled poorly, they move upward into more expensive and stressful territory.

Let's explore each level.

Level 1: Communication and Documentation

The base of the pyramid is the most important level.

This is where the majority of construction issues should be resolved.

At this stage, the contractor and homeowner are still working together and attempting to solve the problem directly.

Typical situations at this level might include:

- a misunderstanding about the scope of work
- a delay in materials or scheduling
- a question about the quality of a specific task
- a disagreement about whether something is included in the contract

When communication remains professional and respectful, most of these problems can be resolved quickly.

For example, a homeowner might believe a certain item was included in the project.

Instead of arguing, the contractor can simply refer to the written contract and explain the scope of work.

Or perhaps a contractor encounters an unexpected condition during the project.

By documenting the situation with photos and explaining the issue clearly, the contractor can request a change order and keep the project moving forward.

This is why **documentation is one of the most powerful tools in construction dispute prevention.**

Photos, written messages, and clear contracts create a record of what was agreed upon.

When both sides can see the facts clearly, disagreements often disappear.

Unfortunately, many contractors rely on verbal agreements or casual text messages.

This can create confusion later when the project does not match someone's expectations.

When communication and documentation break down, the dispute begins moving upward in the pyramid.

Level 2: Mediation and Negotiation

The second level of the pyramid is where outside assistance becomes helpful.

At this stage, the contractor and homeowner are having difficulty resolving the issue directly.

The disagreement has grown more serious.

Trust may have started to erode.

But the parties still want to avoid the cost and stress of a lawsuit.

This is where **mediation** becomes extremely valuable.

Mediation involves a neutral third party who helps both sides discuss the problem and work toward a mutually acceptable solution.

Unlike a judge, the mediator does not make decisions.

Instead, the mediator guides the conversation and helps both sides explore possible compromises.

Mediation works because it shifts the conversation away from accusations and toward practical solutions.

Instead of arguing about who is right or wrong, both sides begin asking:

"What outcome can we both live with?"

Many construction disputes can be resolved through mediation.

For example:

- a contractor might agree to complete a small additional repair
- a homeowner might agree to release a partial payment
- both sides might agree to adjust the project scope

The key advantage of mediation is flexibility.

The parties remain in control of the outcome.

They can create solutions that courts might not even consider.

Mediation also protects relationships.

A contractor who resolves a dispute professionally can preserve their reputation and even maintain goodwill with the client.

In contrast, when disputes escalate further, the process becomes much more rigid and expensive.

Level 3: Litigation

The top of the pyramid represents the most serious stage of a construction dispute.

This is where the conflict enters the legal system.

Litigation can involve:

- small claims court
- civil lawsuits
- contractor licensing board complaints
- mechanic's lien foreclosure actions

Once a dispute reaches this level, the situation changes dramatically.

The focus shifts away from cooperation and toward legal strategy.

Each side begins gathering evidence.

Attorneys may become involved.

Deadlines, filings, and legal procedures begin to control the process.

Litigation can take months or even years to resolve.

It is also expensive.

Legal fees, court costs, and lost time can add significant financial pressure to both parties.

For contractors, litigation can also affect their professional reputation.

Complaints filed with licensing boards or negative public disputes can harm a business even if the contractor ultimately wins the case.

This is why experienced professionals try to resolve disputes **before they reach the top of the pyramid.**

Why the Pyramid Matters

The Construction Dispute Pyramid is not just a theory.

It reflects the real way disputes develop in the construction industry.

Most problems begin at the bottom of the pyramid.

When handled properly, they stay there.

But when communication fails, disputes climb higher and become more destructive.

Understanding the pyramid helps contractors and homeowners recognize warning signs early.

If communication becomes tense, it is time to slow down and document the situation.

If direct discussions are failing, mediation may help restore progress.

The earlier a dispute is addressed, the easier it is to resolve.

The Goal: Keep Disputes Low on the Pyramid

The true purpose of the Construction Dispute Pyramid is simple:

Keep problems at the lowest level possible.

Strong communication, clear contracts, and proper documentation prevent most disputes from escalating.

When disagreements do occur, mediation provides a structured environment to find solutions.

Only when all other options fail should a dispute move into litigation.

Contractors who understand this framework gain a powerful advantage.

Instead of reacting emotionally to conflict, they can respond strategically.

They recognize where the dispute sits within the pyramid and take the appropriate steps to resolve it.

In the next chapter, we will explore another important element of construction disputes:

the psychology of contractors and homeowners.

Understanding how each side thinks—and why their expectations are often very different—can prevent many conflicts before they even begin.

Chapter 3

The Psychology of Contractors and Homeowners

Most construction disputes are not really about drywall, paint, tile, or lumber.

They are about **people**.

Two different worlds collide during a construction project:

- the **contractor's world**
- the **homeowner's world**

Both sides often start with the same goal: to complete a successful project.

But they see the project through completely different lenses.

Understanding this psychological difference is one of the most powerful tools for preventing disputes.

When contractors learn to recognize how homeowners think—and when homeowners understand the pressures contractors face—many conflicts can be avoided before they even begin.

The Contractor's Mindset

For contractors, construction is a profession.

It is a system of schedules, materials, labor, and logistics.

A contractor might be managing:

- several projects at once
- multiple subcontractors
- material deliveries
- inspections
- unexpected repairs

Every day on a job site brings new problems to solve.

Weather delays a project.

A supplier runs out of materials.

A subcontractor calls in sick.

A piece of equipment breaks.

To a contractor, these challenges are normal.

They are simply part of the construction process.

Contractors learn to adapt quickly and keep moving forward.

But this practical mindset can sometimes create a communication gap with homeowners.

Contractors often assume that homeowners understand the complexity of construction.

In reality, many homeowners have never been involved in a major renovation project before.

What seems routine to a contractor may feel alarming to a homeowner.

The Homeowner's Perspective

For homeowners, a construction project is rarely routine.

It may be the largest investment they make in their property.

Sometimes it involves money they have saved for years.

Sometimes it involves a loan they will spend decades repaying.

The home itself also carries emotional meaning.

It is where families live, raise children, and create memories.

When construction begins, homeowners may feel excitement—but they may also feel anxiety.

Questions quickly arise:

Will the project stay on budget?

Will it be finished on time?

Will the final result match what they imagined?

When something unexpected happens, even a small issue can feel like a major problem.

A homeowner who sees dust, delays, or incomplete work may worry that the project is going wrong.

Without clear communication, that worry can grow into suspicion or frustration.

Different Definitions of "Done"

Another psychological difference between contractors and homeowners involves the idea of **completion**.

Contractors often view a project through a technical lens.

If the work meets industry standards and the contract requirements, the job is considered complete.

Homeowners, however, may evaluate the project through a visual or emotional lens.

They may notice small details that bother them:

A brush stroke they didn't expect.

A piece of trim that doesn't look perfectly aligned.

A color that appears different under certain lighting.

To the contractor, these may be minor cosmetic issues.

To the homeowner, they may feel like signs that the project was not done correctly.

This difference in perception can create frustration on both sides.

The contractor may feel the homeowner is being unreasonable.

The homeowner may feel the contractor is ignoring their concerns.

Understanding that these perceptions come from different perspectives can help both sides communicate more effectively.

The Fear Factor

Many homeowners carry an underlying fear during construction projects.

They may have heard stories about contractors who disappeared with deposits.

They may know someone who had a renovation go terribly wrong.

They may worry about being taken advantage of.

Even when the contractor is honest and professional, these fears can influence how the homeowner interprets events.

A delayed response to a message might feel suspicious.

An unexpected cost might feel like dishonesty.

This fear can cause homeowners to become defensive or confrontational.

From the contractor's perspective, this behavior may seem unfair.

But understanding the source of that fear can help contractors respond calmly and professionally.

Clear communication and documentation are powerful tools for reducing homeowner anxiety.

The Contractor's Frustration

Contractors also experience their own frustrations during disputes.

Running a construction business is demanding.

Margins are often thin.

Projects require careful coordination.

When a homeowner questions the work repeatedly or delays payments, contractors may feel that their professionalism is being challenged.

They may begin to feel that their effort and expertise are not being respected.

This frustration can lead to defensive responses or strained communication.

Unfortunately, when both sides become defensive, the situation escalates quickly.

What began as a simple misunderstanding can turn into a serious conflict.

The Escalation Cycle

Many construction disputes follow a predictable psychological cycle.

1. **A small problem occurs.**

Perhaps a detail was overlooked or a timeline shifts slightly.

1. **Assumptions are made.**

The homeowner assumes the contractor is careless.
The contractor assumes the homeowner is unreasonable.

1. **Communication becomes tense.**

Messages become shorter and more defensive.

1. **Trust begins to break down.**

Both sides start preparing to protect themselves rather than solve the problem together.

1. **The dispute escalates.**

Legal threats, complaints, or payment disputes may follow.

Recognizing this cycle early is extremely important.

Once trust begins to break down, resolving the dispute becomes much more difficult.

The Professional Advantage

Professional contractors understand that construction is not just about building structures.

It is about managing relationships.

A contractor who communicates clearly, documents work carefully, and remains calm during difficult conversations gains a significant advantage.

Homeowners also benefit when they approach the project with realistic expectations and open communication.

When both sides understand the psychological pressures involved, they can avoid many unnecessary conflicts.

In the next chapter, we will examine how construction disputes actually develop step by step.

By understanding the anatomy of a dispute, contractors and homeowners can recognize warning signs early—

Chapter 4

The Anatomy of a Construction Dispute

Construction disputes rarely begin with shouting, legal threats, or court filings.

They almost always begin with something small.

A simple misunderstanding.

A missed phone call.

An unclear expectation.

At the beginning, the issue may seem minor. Often both sides assume the problem will work itself out.

But when the situation is not addressed early, the problem slowly grows. Communication breaks down, trust erodes, and what started as a simple issue turns into a serious conflict.

Understanding how this process works is critical for both contractors and homeowners.

Once you can recognize the stages of a dispute, you can stop the escalation before it reaches the most destructive levels.

Stage 1: The Small Problem

Every dispute begins with a small problem.

It might be something like:

- a change in the scope of work
- a delay in materials
- a misunderstanding about the contract
- a cosmetic issue noticed by the homeowner

In most cases, neither side intends for the situation to become a conflict.

But if the issue is ignored or poorly communicated, it becomes the seed of a larger problem.

For example, a homeowner might notice something they do not like about the work.

Instead of addressing it immediately, they may wait to see if it improves.

At the same time, the contractor may believe the work is progressing normally.

Because the issue was never clearly discussed, both sides continue forward with different assumptions.

Stage 2: The Assumption

When a problem is not addressed directly, both sides begin filling in the missing information themselves.

This is where assumptions begin to form.

The homeowner might think:

"Why hasn't the contractor fixed this yet?"

The contractor might think:

"Why hasn't the homeowner said anything if there is a problem?"

Neither side realizes that the other is interpreting the situation differently.

Assumptions are dangerous because they replace facts with speculation.

Once assumptions take hold, emotions often begin to influence the situation.

Stage 3: The Communication Breakdown

Eventually the issue becomes difficult to ignore.

The homeowner raises the concern.

But by this time frustration may already exist.

Instead of a calm discussion, the conversation may feel tense.

The homeowner may express dissatisfaction.

The contractor may feel that the criticism is unfair.

Both sides begin focusing on defending their position rather than understanding the other perspective.

Communication becomes shorter and less cooperative.

Messages may be delayed or avoided.

At this stage, the relationship between contractor and homeowner begins to weaken.

Stage 4: The Documentation Battle

Once communication breaks down, both sides often begin documenting the situation more carefully.

Photos are taken.

Text messages are saved.

Emails become more formal.

Instead of working together to complete the project, each side begins protecting themselves.

The homeowner might research contractor complaint procedures.

The contractor might start reviewing the contract to confirm what was agreed upon.

This stage often marks a turning point in the dispute.

If the issue can still be resolved through calm discussion or mediation, the project may recover.

If not, the conflict continues to escalate.

Stage 5: Payment Tension

One of the most common moments when disputes intensify involves payment.

Construction projects typically involve several payment stages.

When a disagreement exists, those payments can become leverage.

A homeowner might withhold payment until the issue is resolved.

A contractor might pause work until payment is received.

Both sides may believe they are acting reasonably.

The homeowner wants assurance that the work will meet expectations.

The contractor wants assurance that they will be paid for the work already completed.

Unfortunately, when payment becomes a tool in the dispute, emotions often rise quickly.

Trust begins to collapse.

Stage 6: The Threat

When frustration reaches a certain point, the language of the conversation changes.

Legal threats begin to appear.

A homeowner may mention filing a complaint.

A contractor may mention liens or legal rights.

At this stage, both sides are no longer focused on finishing the project.

They are focused on **protecting themselves and gaining leverage**.

The dispute has now reached a dangerous stage.

If nothing interrupts this escalation, the next step is often legal action.

Stage 7: Formal Dispute

The final stage of the dispute occurs when the conflict enters a formal system.

This may involve:

- a complaint filed with a contractor licensing board
- a small claims lawsuit
- a civil court case
- a mechanic's lien

Once a dispute reaches this stage, it becomes much more complex and expensive.

Legal procedures replace normal conversation.

Deadlines and filings control the timeline.

Both sides may spend significant time and money pursuing a resolution.

Even when the dispute is eventually resolved, the relationship between the contractor and homeowner is often permanently damaged.

Why Understanding This Process Matters

The anatomy of a construction dispute reveals an important truth:

Most conflicts escalate gradually.

There are many opportunities along the way to stop the problem from growing.

A calm conversation during the early stages can prevent months of conflict later.

Clear documentation can resolve misunderstandings before they escalate.

Professional communication can restore trust before legal threats appear.

Contractors who understand this process gain an important advantage.

Instead of reacting emotionally when problems arise, they can recognize which stage the dispute has reached and respond appropriately.

Homeowners benefit from this knowledge as well.

Recognizing the early signs of conflict allows them to address concerns before the project relationship deteriorates.

In the next chapter, we will explore one of the most powerful tools for preventing disputes altogether:

clear communication on the job site.

Many construction conflicts never need to happen at all when communication is handled properly from the beginning.

and prevent small problems from turning into major legal battles.

Chapter 5

Communication on the Job Site

If there is one skill that separates successful contractors from those who constantly struggle with disputes, it is **communication**.

Construction is often viewed as a technical trade. People imagine contractors working with tools, materials, and equipment.

But in reality, much of the job involves managing conversations.

Contractors communicate with:

- homeowners
- subcontractors
- suppliers
- inspectors
- crew members

Every project is built on hundreds of small interactions.

When those interactions are clear and professional, projects move smoothly.

When communication breaks down, misunderstandings grow quickly.

Many construction disputes that eventually reach licensing boards or courtrooms could have been prevented with better communication at the beginning of the project.

The Danger of Assumptions

One of the biggest communication mistakes in construction is assuming that everyone understands the same thing.

Contractors may believe the homeowner understands the scope of work.

Homeowners may believe the contractor understands exactly how they want the final result to look.

But unless those expectations are clearly discussed and documented, assumptions fill the gap.

For example, a homeowner might say:

"I want the walls to look perfect."

To the homeowner, this may mean a flawless finish.

To the contractor, it may mean a professional paint job that meets industry standards.

Both sides think they are communicating clearly.

But their definitions of "perfect" may be very different.

Clear communication removes these assumptions before they turn into problems.

Setting Expectations Early

One of the most important moments in any construction project happens before the work even begins.

This is when expectations are established.

A professional contractor should explain:

- what work will be performed
- what work is not included
- the expected timeline
- the payment structure
- how change orders will be handled

When homeowners understand the structure of the project from the beginning, they feel more comfortable and confident.

It also reduces the chance that unexpected requests will appear later.

Expectations should never be left to casual conversation alone.

They should be supported by clear written agreements.

The Power of Written Communication

In today's construction environment, much communication happens through text messages and email.

While these tools are convenient, they can also create confusion if used casually.

Professional contractors treat written communication as part of their documentation system.

Important discussions should be summarized in writing.

For example, if a homeowner requests additional work, the contractor might send a message like this:

"Just confirming our conversation today. You asked us to repaint the hallway ceiling as well. This work is not included in the original contract, but we can add it as a change order."

This type of message accomplishes several things.

It confirms the conversation.

It clarifies the scope of work.

And it creates a written record of the agreement.

When written communication becomes part of the project system, many misunderstandings disappear.

Regular Project Updates

Another communication strategy that prevents disputes is providing regular updates.

Homeowners often feel anxious when they do not know what is happening on their project.

Silence can create unnecessary worry.

A simple update message can make a big difference.

For example:

"Today we completed the second coat of paint in the living room. Tomorrow we will begin the trim work."

This kind of communication keeps the homeowner informed and reassured.

It also demonstrates professionalism and organization.

Homeowners who feel informed are far less likely to assume that something is going wrong.

Handling Concerns Professionally

Even on well-managed projects, concerns will occasionally arise.

A homeowner may notice something they do not like.

When this happens, the contractor's response is extremely important.

Defensive reactions often make the situation worse.

Instead of arguing immediately, professional contractors listen carefully to the concern.

They acknowledge the homeowner's perspective and evaluate the situation calmly.

A simple response might be:

"Thank you for pointing that out. Let's take a closer look together and see what we can do."

This type of response keeps the conversation productive rather than confrontational.

Even if the contractor ultimately believes the work meets industry standards, addressing the concern respectfully helps maintain trust.

Avoiding Emotional Escalation

Construction projects can become emotional, especially when unexpected problems occur.

Contractors may feel frustrated by repeated questions.

Homeowners may feel anxious about delays or costs.

If both sides allow emotions to control the conversation, the situation can escalate quickly.

Professional communication requires staying calm even when tensions rise.

This means focusing on facts rather than accusations.

Instead of saying:

"You never told me that."

A more productive approach might be:

"Let's review the contract together and make sure we're both on the same page."

This approach shifts the conversation from conflict to problem-solving.

Communication as a Business System

Successful contractors treat communication as part of their business system.

They develop consistent habits such as:

- documenting conversations
- confirming changes in writing
- providing regular updates
- responding to concerns professionally

These habits create a clear record of the project and reduce misunderstandings.

They also demonstrate professionalism, which builds trust with clients.

Contractors who develop strong communication systems often experience fewer disputes and stronger reputations.

Communication and Reputation

In today's connected world, reputation travels quickly.

Homeowners share their experiences online.

Reviews and recommendations influence future clients.

Contractors who communicate clearly and respectfully—even during difficult situations—build a reputation for professionalism.

That reputation becomes one of the most valuable assets in the construction business.

On the other hand, contractors who allow disputes to escalate through poor communication may find their reputation damaged, even if the dispute itself was minor.

Strong communication protects not only the project, but the long-term success of the business.

The Foundation of Dispute Prevention

Clear communication is one of the strongest defenses against construction disputes.

When expectations are explained, conversations are documented, and concerns are addressed professionally, most conflicts can be resolved before they grow.

Communication works best when it is supported by another powerful tool:

documentation.

In the next chapter, we will explore how photos, records, and written documentation can protect contractors and homeowners when disagreements arise.

Because in construction, the simple rule is often true:

the best documentation wins the argument.

Chapter 6

Documentation: The Contractor's Best Defense

There is a simple truth that experienced contractors eventually learn:

The best documentation usually wins the argument.

When construction disputes arise, memories become unreliable. Conversations are remembered differently. Expectations shift. Each side begins telling their version of the story.

But documentation tells the story with facts.

Photos.

Messages.

Contracts.

Invoices.

These records create a timeline of the project that cannot easily be disputed.

For contractors and homeowners alike, proper documentation is one of the most powerful tools for preventing misunderstandings and resolving disputes.

Why Documentation Matters

Construction projects involve many moving parts.

Multiple conversations occur throughout the project.

Changes are requested.

Materials are selected.

Schedules are adjusted.

Without documentation, these details can quickly become unclear.

A homeowner might believe a certain item was included in the project.

A contractor might believe it was never discussed.

Without a written record, the disagreement becomes a matter of opinion.

But when documentation exists, the facts become much easier to determine.

For example:

• A photo can show the condition of the work before and after a repair.

• A message can confirm that a change order was requested.

• A written contract can define exactly what work was included.

Documentation removes guesswork from the dispute.

The Documentation Mindset

Many contractors only begin documenting a project when a problem appears.

By that time, important information may already be missing.

Professional contractors take a different approach.

They treat documentation as a normal part of every project from the beginning.

This mindset creates a clear record of the entire job.

It also discourages disputes before they even begin.

When homeowners see that a contractor keeps detailed records and communicates clearly, they understand that the project is being managed professionally.

Jobsite Photography

One of the simplest and most powerful forms of documentation is photography.

Modern smartphones make it easy to document the condition of a project at every stage.

Contractors should take photos:

• before work begins

• during key stages of the project

- after work is completed

These photos serve several important purposes.

They document the original condition of the property.

They show the progress of the work.

They provide visual evidence of the finished project.

If a dispute arises later, these images can provide clear proof of what occurred.

For example, if a homeowner claims that damage occurred during construction, photos taken before the project began may show that the issue already existed.

Likewise, progress photos can demonstrate that the work was performed according to plan.

Written Communication Records

Text messages and emails have become common tools for communication in construction projects.

These messages can also serve as valuable documentation.

Whenever important discussions occur, it is wise to confirm them in writing.

For example:

"Just confirming our conversation today. You asked us to add an additional coat of paint to the kitchen cabinets. This will be included as a change order."

This type of message creates a clear record of the conversation.

It ensures that both sides understand the agreement.

And if confusion arises later, the written record can clarify what was discussed.

Contractors should avoid relying solely on verbal agreements whenever possible.

Verbal agreements are easy to misunderstand and difficult to prove.

Written confirmation protects everyone involved.

Change Orders

One of the most common sources of construction disputes involves changes to the project.

Homeowners frequently request additional work after the project begins.

Sometimes the request seems minor.

But even small changes can affect the schedule, cost, or scope of the project.

This is why professional contractors use **change orders**.

A change order is a written agreement that describes:

- the additional work requested
- the cost of the change
- the effect on the project timeline

By documenting the change before the work begins, both sides understand exactly what is being added to the project.

Without a change order, the situation can quickly become confusing.

The homeowner may believe the work was included in the original agreement.

The contractor may believe it was an additional request.

Change orders eliminate that confusion.

Daily Jobsite Notes

Some contractors take documentation a step further by keeping simple daily jobsite notes.

These notes do not need to be complicated.

They might include information such as:

- work completed that day
- materials delivered
- weather conditions

• conversations with the homeowner

These notes create a timeline of the project.

If a dispute arises months later, the contractor can review the notes and remember exactly what occurred.

Daily notes can also demonstrate professionalism and organization.

They show that the contractor manages projects carefully and systematically.

Payment Records

Another critical form of documentation involves payment records.

Contractors should maintain clear records of:

• deposits received

• progress payments

• final payments

Invoices and receipts provide proof that payments were made according to the agreement.

If payment disputes occur later, these records can clarify the financial history of the project.

Homeowners benefit from these records as well.

Clear payment documentation ensures that both sides understand the financial structure of the project.

Documentation Protects Both Sides

Although documentation often benefits contractors during disputes, it is important to remember that it protects homeowners as well.

Homeowners who keep records of contracts, invoices, and communications can demonstrate their concerns clearly if a dispute occurs.

Good documentation creates transparency.

It allows both sides to focus on facts rather than speculation.

In many cases, simply reviewing the documented record of a project can resolve disagreements quickly.

The Professional Advantage

Contractors who develop strong documentation habits gain a significant advantage in the construction industry.

They reduce misunderstandings.

They protect themselves during disputes.

And they demonstrate professionalism to their clients.

Documentation does not need to be complicated.

It simply needs to be consistent.

Photos, written confirmations, change orders, and payment records together create a powerful system of protection.

In the next chapter, we will move from dispute prevention into the process of **mediation preparation**.

When disputes cannot be resolved through communication and documentation alone, mediation offers a structured way for both sides to work toward a practical resolution.

Chapter 7

Preparing for Mediation

Even with strong communication and careful documentation, some construction disputes still reach a point where the contractor and homeowner cannot resolve the issue on their own.

At this stage, continuing to argue rarely solves the problem.

Both sides become frustrated.

Conversations repeat the same points.

Trust begins to weaken.

This is where **mediation** becomes one of the most valuable tools in construction dispute resolution.

Mediation allows both sides to step away from the emotional tension of the job site and discuss the problem in a structured environment with the help of a neutral third party.

But mediation works best when both parties arrive prepared.

Preparation helps the mediator understand the situation quickly and allows both sides to present their concerns clearly.

In this chapter, we will explore how contractors and homeowners should prepare for mediation and what information should be organized before entering the mediation process.

What Mediation Is — and What It Is Not

Before preparing for mediation, it is important to understand what mediation actually involves.

Mediation is **not a courtroom**.

There is no judge deciding who is right or wrong.

Instead, mediation is a guided negotiation process led by a neutral mediator whose role is to help both sides communicate and explore possible solutions.

The mediator does not impose a decision.

Instead, the mediator helps the parties reach their own agreement.

This flexibility is one of the reasons mediation works so well for construction disputes.

Construction conflicts often involve practical solutions that a court might not consider.

For example, mediation may result in:

- an agreement to complete additional work
- a negotiated payment plan
- a partial refund or adjustment
- a mutually agreed project modification

Because both sides participate in creating the solution, the final agreement often feels more fair and workable than a court decision.

Organizing the Dispute File

The most important step in preparing for mediation is organizing the **dispute file**.

This file contains the documents and information that explain what happened during the project.

Both contractors and homeowners should gather the following materials.

The Contract

The contract is the foundation of the project.

It defines:

- the scope of work
- payment terms
- timelines
- responsibilities of each party

During mediation, the contract often becomes the starting point for evaluating the dispute.

The mediator will want to understand exactly what work was originally agreed upon.

Change Orders

If the project involved changes after the contract was signed, those changes should be documented with written change orders.

These documents show how the scope of the project evolved.

Without change orders, disagreements about additional work can become difficult to resolve.

Communication Records

Emails, text messages, and written correspondence often reveal how the project developed.

These records can show:

- when concerns were raised
- how each side responded
- what agreements were made during the project

Organizing communication records chronologically can help the mediator understand the sequence of events.

Jobsite Photos

Photographs provide visual evidence of the work performed.

Photos may show:

- the condition of the property before work began
- progress during the project
- the final condition of the work

In many cases, a photo can clarify a situation much faster than a lengthy explanation.

Payment History

A clear record of payments is also important.

Both sides should be able to show:

- deposits paid
- progress payments made
- invoices issued
- any outstanding balances

Payment records often play a central role in construction disputes.

Having these records organized helps the mediator understand the financial status of the project.

Clarifying the Core Issue

Another important step in mediation preparation is identifying the **core issue** of the dispute.

Many construction conflicts involve several smaller disagreements that developed over time.

But beneath those details, there is usually one central problem.

For example:

- disagreement about the quality of work
- disagreement about the scope of the contract
- disagreement about payment

Understanding the core issue helps both sides focus their discussion during mediation.

Without this clarity, mediation sessions can become confusing or unproductive.

Preparing Your Position

Each party should also take time to prepare a clear explanation of their position.

This explanation should focus on facts rather than emotions.

Instead of saying:

"This whole project was a disaster."

It is more helpful to explain:

"The homeowner requested additional work in three areas that were not included in the original contract."

Clear, factual explanations help the mediator understand the situation quickly.

They also help the discussion remain constructive.

Being Open to Solutions

Successful mediation requires a willingness to explore solutions.

If both sides enter mediation determined only to prove that they are right, the process becomes difficult.

The goal of mediation is not to determine a winner and a loser.

The goal is to find a resolution that both sides can accept.

This often requires compromise.

For contractors, compromise might involve completing a small additional repair or adjusting the payment structure.

For homeowners, compromise might involve recognizing that certain expectations were outside the scope of the contract.

Flexibility allows mediation to succeed where rigid arguments often fail.

The Benefits of Preparation

When both parties arrive at mediation organized and prepared, the process becomes far more effective.

Preparation allows the mediator to focus on resolving the dispute rather than trying to understand what happened.

It also helps both sides communicate their concerns clearly.

Well-prepared mediation sessions often lead to faster resolutions and lower costs for everyone involved.

In the next chapter, we will explore what actually happens during mediation itself.

Understanding **how the mediation room works** can remove much of the uncertainty and anxiety surrounding the process.

Chapter 8

Inside the Mediation Room

For many contractors and homeowners, mediation feels mysterious.

They may imagine something similar to a courtroom, where each side argues their case while a decision-maker determines who is right and who is wrong.

But mediation works very differently.

It is not about winning a legal battle.

It is about finding a practical solution that both sides can live with.

Understanding what happens during mediation can remove much of the anxiety surrounding the process and help both parties participate more effectively.

The Purpose of Mediation

The primary goal of mediation is simple:

Resolve the dispute without going to court.

Construction disputes can become extremely expensive and time-consuming once they enter the legal system.

Attorneys become involved.

Court procedures create delays.

Costs increase for everyone.

Mediation offers a more efficient path.

Instead of fighting in a courtroom, both parties sit down with a neutral mediator who helps guide the conversation toward a resolution.

The mediator's role is not to determine who wins.

The mediator's role is to help both sides communicate and explore practical solutions.

In construction disputes, this is particularly valuable because many problems are not strictly legal—they are practical.

They may involve unfinished work, payment disagreements, or misunderstandings about the project scope.

These issues are often better solved through negotiation than through a courtroom judgment.

The Role of the Mediator

The mediator acts as a **neutral facilitator**.

They do not represent either party.

They do not provide legal advice.

They do not make legal decisions.

Instead, they help structure the conversation so that it remains productive and focused.

A skilled mediator listens carefully to both sides and helps clarify the issues involved.

They may ask questions such as:

- What was originally agreed upon in the contract?
- What part of the project caused the disagreement?
- What outcome would each side consider acceptable?

These questions help both parties shift their thinking away from accusations and toward possible solutions.

Another important role of the mediator is managing emotional tension.

Construction disputes can become personal, especially when large amounts of money or time have been invested in a project.

A mediator creates a controlled environment where the discussion remains calm and respectful.

The Confidential Nature of Mediation

One of the most important principles of mediation is **confidentiality**.

Mediation sessions are generally private and confidential.

This means that statements made during mediation usually cannot be used later in court.

This protection allows both parties to speak more openly during the process.

For example, a contractor might be willing to discuss possible compromises without worrying that those statements will later be used against them in litigation.

Likewise, a homeowner may feel more comfortable expressing concerns honestly in a confidential setting.

Confidentiality encourages honest conversation and helps the parties explore solutions without fear of legal consequences.

This is one reason mediation often succeeds where traditional negotiations fail.

The Opening Discussion

Most mediation sessions begin with an opening discussion.

Both parties are given an opportunity to explain their perspective on the dispute.

This is not a debate.

Each side speaks while the other listens.

The mediator may summarize the key points to ensure that everyone understands the issues clearly.

For example:

A contractor might explain that additional work was requested after the original contract was signed.

A homeowner might explain that they believed the work was included in the project.

Often this is the first time each side has had the opportunity to explain their position fully in a structured environment.

Sometimes this alone reveals misunderstandings that were never properly addressed during the project itself.

Caucus Sessions

After the initial discussion, many mediators move into what are called **caucus sessions.**

A caucus is a private meeting between the mediator and one party.

The other party waits in a separate room while this discussion takes place.

Caucuses are extremely valuable because they allow each party to speak more freely.

During a caucus, the mediator may explore questions such as:

- What outcome would you realistically accept?
- What concerns do you have about continuing the dispute?
- What risks do you see if the case goes to court?
- What compromises might be possible?

Because caucus conversations are confidential, the mediator cannot share information from one side to the other unless permission is given.

This allows the mediator to understand each party's true concerns and priorities.

The mediator then moves back and forth between the parties, gradually exploring possible solutions.

This process is sometimes called **shuttle diplomacy**, because the mediator carries ideas and proposals between the two sides.

Exploring Solutions

Once the mediator understands the positions of both parties, the mediation shifts toward finding a resolution.

Construction disputes often involve practical solutions rather than strict legal rulings.

Possible outcomes may include:

- completing additional repairs
- adjusting the project scope
- agreeing on a partial payment

- creating a payment plan
- modifying the project timeline
- walking away from the project with a settlement agreement

Because mediation allows flexibility, the parties can create solutions that address the specific circumstances of the dispute.

Courts are limited to legal rulings.

Mediation allows the parties to design their own agreement.

This flexibility is one of the greatest strengths of the mediation process.

The Settlement Agreement

If the parties reach an agreement during mediation, the terms are written down in a **settlement agreement**.

This document clearly describes the resolution so that both sides understand their responsibilities.

For example, the agreement might state:

- what work will be completed
- how much payment will be made
- the timeline for completing the agreement
- when the project will be considered finished

Once both parties sign the settlement agreement, it becomes a binding resolution to the dispute.

Many construction conflicts end successfully at this stage.

Both sides avoid the cost and stress of litigation and are able to move forward.

When Mediation Does Not Resolve the Dispute

Although mediation is highly effective, not every dispute reaches a settlement.

Sometimes the parties remain too far apart in their expectations.

When mediation does not produce an agreement, the dispute may move to the next level of resolution.

This could involve:

- filing a complaint with a contractor licensing board
- pursuing a small claims case
- initiating a civil lawsuit
- enforcing a mechanic's lien

Even when mediation does not completely resolve the dispute, it often provides valuable insight.

Both sides gain a clearer understanding of the strengths and weaknesses of their position.

That information alone often leads to settlement later.

The Value of Mediation

Mediation works because it changes the structure of the conflict.

Instead of fighting over who is right, the parties begin working toward a solution.

Contractors benefit because mediation is usually faster and less expensive than litigation.

Homeowners benefit because mediation allows them to address concerns without entering a lengthy legal process.

Most importantly, mediation allows both sides to retain control over the outcome.

Rather than having a judge decide the future of the dispute, the parties create their own resolution.

In the next chapter, we will explore **settlement strategies**—the negotiation approaches that often lead to successful resolutions in construction disputes.

Understanding how settlements work can help both contractors and homeowners reach agreements that allow them to move forward and avoid prolonged conflict.

Chapter 9

Settlement Strategies

How Construction Disputes Actually Get Resolved

Most construction disputes do not end in court.

In fact, the vast majority are resolved through negotiation and settlement.

This is true whether the dispute happens during mediation, during a licensing complaint, or even after a lawsuit has been filed.

Why?

Because litigation is expensive.

It takes time.

It creates uncertainty.

And the final decision is placed in the hands of someone who was never present during the project.

For both contractors and homeowners, settlement often becomes the most practical solution.

But successful settlement rarely happens by accident.

It requires understanding how negotiation works and how leverage influences the outcome of a dispute.

The Goal of Settlement

When people first enter a dispute, they often focus on proving that they are right.

But settlement works differently.

The goal of settlement is not to prove a point.

The goal is to **solve the problem in a way that both sides can accept.**

This means each party must evaluate the situation realistically.

Contractors may need to ask:

- Is continuing the dispute worth the time and stress?
- Would completing a small repair resolve the conflict quickly?

Homeowners may need to ask:

- Is the disagreement worth months of legal conflict?
- Would a partial adjustment resolve the issue and allow the project to move forward?

Once both sides shift from proving a point to solving the problem, resolution becomes much more likely.

The Contractor Payment Triangle

One of the most useful ways to understand construction disputes is through a concept I call the:

Contractor Payment Triangle

Three elements determine the strength of a contractor's position in a dispute:

Contract

Documentation

Leverage

When all three are strong, the contractor stands on solid ground.

Contract

The contract defines the agreement between the parties.

It outlines:

- the scope of work
- payment terms
- timelines
- responsibilities

A clear contract becomes the foundation of the contractor's position during a dispute.

When a disagreement occurs, the first question often becomes:

"What does the contract say?"

Documentation

Documentation supports the contract.

Photos, messages, change orders, and invoices create a record of what actually occurred during the project.

Documentation helps answer important questions such as:

- Was additional work requested?
- Was the homeowner informed of the change?
- Was the work completed according to the agreement?

Strong documentation can resolve many disputes quickly because it replaces speculation with evidence.

Leverage

The third element of the triangle is leverage.

Leverage refers to the practical pressure points that influence negotiation.

In construction disputes, leverage may include:

- unpaid balances
- the ability to file a mechanic's lien
- licensing board complaints
- the cost of litigation

Both contractors and homeowners possess certain forms of leverage.

Understanding these forces helps explain why settlements occur.

When both sides recognize the risks of continuing the dispute, compromise becomes more attractive.

Common Settlement Structures

Construction disputes are resolved in several common ways.

Understanding these structures can help both parties explore practical solutions during mediation or negotiation.

Partial Payment Agreements

One common resolution involves a partial payment.

The homeowner may agree to release part of the outstanding payment, while the contractor agrees to close the dispute.

This approach allows both sides to move forward without extended conflict.

Repair Agreements

Sometimes the dispute centers around specific work that the homeowner believes was not completed properly.

In these cases, a settlement may involve the contractor returning to complete repairs or adjustments.

This solution can satisfy the homeowner while preserving the contractor's reputation.

Scope Adjustments

Another option involves adjusting the scope of the project.

For example, the contractor may agree to remove a portion of the work while the homeowner agrees to reduce the payment accordingly.

This approach recognizes that expectations changed during the project.

Payment Plans

In some cases, the homeowner may owe money but cannot pay the full amount immediately.

A payment plan allows the homeowner to resolve the balance over time while avoiding litigation.

Walk-Away Settlements

Sometimes the best resolution is for both parties to separate and move forward.

In these situations, both sides agree to end the project relationship and release each other from further claims.

Although this may feel unsatisfying, it often saves both sides significant time and expense.

The Power of Professionalism

One of the most effective negotiation tools is professionalism.

Contractors who remain calm, organized, and respectful during disputes gain credibility.

Mediators, licensing boards, and courts often pay attention to which party appears reasonable.

A contractor who presents clear documentation and communicates professionally often gains a significant advantage.

Likewise, homeowners who approach disputes calmly and focus on facts often achieve better outcomes than those who rely on emotion or accusations.

Professional behavior signals that the party is focused on resolution rather than conflict.

Knowing When to Settle

One of the most difficult decisions in any dispute is knowing when to settle.

Sometimes the strongest strategy is to continue pursuing the claim.

Other times, settlement is the wiser choice.

Experienced contractors learn to evaluate disputes pragmatically.

They consider factors such as:

- the strength of the documentation
- the potential cost of litigation
- the time required to resolve the case
- the impact on their business reputation

When the cost of continuing the dispute outweighs the benefit of winning, settlement often becomes the best option.

The Quiet Reality of Construction Disputes

In the public imagination, disputes often end with dramatic courtroom battles.

In reality, most construction conflicts end quietly through negotiated agreements.

Both sides sign a settlement.

The project ends.

And everyone moves on with their lives.

Understanding how settlements work allows contractors and homeowners to navigate disputes more effectively.

Instead of reacting emotionally, they can evaluate the situation strategically and work toward a resolution.

In the next chapter, we will explore what happens when disputes cannot be resolved through mediation or settlement.

Although litigation is usually the final option, understanding the next steps can help both contractors and homeowners prepare for the realities of the legal process.

Chapter 10

When Mediation Fails

Although mediation is highly effective, not every dispute reaches a settlement.

Sometimes the parties remain too far apart in their expectations.

One side may believe they are completely right.

The other side may refuse to compromise.

When this happens, the dispute moves beyond negotiation and into more formal resolution processes.

This stage represents the **top level of the Construction Dispute Pyramid**.

At this point, the disagreement may enter legal or regulatory systems designed to resolve conflicts when private negotiation fails.

Understanding these options helps contractors and homeowners prepare for what comes next.

Licensing Board Complaints

In many states, contractors operate under a licensing authority that regulates construction professionals.

In California, this authority is the **Contractors State License Board (CSLB).**

Homeowners who believe a contractor violated licensing laws may file a complaint with the board.

These complaints may involve issues such as:

- poor workmanship
- contract violations
- unlicensed contracting
- failure to complete work

When a complaint is filed, the licensing board may investigate the situation.

Investigators may review contracts, photographs, and communication records.

In some cases, the board may attempt to resolve the dispute through its own mediation or settlement process.

If violations are found, disciplinary action may occur.

This could include:

- license suspension
- fines
- mandatory corrections to the work

For contractors, licensing complaints can have serious consequences.

That is why professional communication and documentation throughout the project are so important.

Mechanic's Liens

Another tool that sometimes appears when mediation fails is the **mechanic's lien**.

Mechanic's liens allow contractors, subcontractors, and suppliers to secure payment for work performed on a property.

When properly filed, a lien places a legal claim against the property itself.

This creates pressure to resolve the payment dispute because the property owner cannot easily sell or refinance the property while the lien exists.

Lien law is complex and varies by state, but the basic concept is simple:

If you improve a property and are not paid, you may have the right to claim a security interest in that property.

Mechanic's liens can be powerful leverage during disputes.

However, they must be used carefully and within strict legal deadlines.

We will explore this topic in much greater detail in **Book 3 of this series: Mechanic's Liens Made Simple.**

Civil Lawsuits

When disputes cannot be resolved through negotiation, mediation, or administrative complaints, the next step may involve a civil lawsuit.

Civil lawsuits allow parties to ask a court to determine liability and award damages.

In construction disputes, lawsuits may involve claims such as:

- breach of contract
- property damage
- unpaid work
- construction defects

Civil litigation can be lengthy.

Cases may take months or even years to resolve.

Legal fees, expert witnesses, and court procedures can create significant financial costs for both sides.

This is one reason mediation is strongly encouraged before disputes reach this stage.

Even after a lawsuit begins, many cases still settle before reaching trial.

The Financial Reality of Litigation

One of the most important considerations in any dispute is the cost of pursuing the claim.

Even when a party believes they are completely right, litigation may not always be the most practical option.

Legal fees can quickly exceed the value of the dispute.

Time spent preparing for court may distract from running a business or managing personal responsibilities.

Stress and uncertainty can also take a personal toll.

This is why experienced professionals often evaluate disputes strategically rather than emotionally.

Sometimes the most effective outcome is not winning the argument—it is resolving the problem efficiently and moving forward.

The Professional Advantage

Contractors who understand dispute resolution systems gain a major advantage.

They recognize when communication can solve the problem.

They use mediation when negotiation stalls.

And when necessary, they understand the formal processes that may follow.

This knowledge allows contractors to approach disputes calmly and strategically.

Instead of reacting with frustration, they can evaluate the situation and decide the best path forward.

For homeowners, understanding these systems also provides protection.

It allows them to recognize their rights and resolve disputes through appropriate channels.

Moving Forward

Construction disputes are rarely enjoyable.

But they are a reality of the industry.

The key is not avoiding conflict entirely—that is impossible.

The key is understanding how to navigate conflict professionally and intelligently.

When contractors and homeowners understand the dispute process, they can resolve problems more efficiently and avoid unnecessary escalation.

In the next chapter, we will explore **Small Claims Court**, a system designed to resolve disputes quickly and affordably without the complexity of full civil litigation.

For many construction conflicts, small claims court becomes the final step in achieving resolution.

Chapter 11

Small Claims Court for Contractors and Homeowners

When disputes cannot be resolved through communication, mediation, or settlement, the next step may be **small claims court.**

Small claims court exists for one primary reason:

To resolve disputes quickly and affordably without requiring lawyers.

For many construction disagreements—especially those involving residential projects—small claims court becomes the final place where the dispute is decided.

Unlike traditional civil court, small claims procedures are designed for ordinary people.

Contractors, homeowners, and small business owners can present their cases directly to a judge.

Because lawyers are usually not involved, the focus of the case becomes simple:

Who has the clearest facts and the strongest documentation?

This is where preparation becomes extremely important.

When Small Claims Is Used

Small claims court is commonly used for disputes involving:

- unpaid construction work
- incomplete or defective work
- property damage claims
- deposit disputes
- payment disagreements between contractors and homeowners

In many states, small claims courts have limits on the amount of money that can be requested.

For example, in California:

- individuals may claim up to **$10,000**
- businesses may claim up to **$5,000**

These limits make small claims court ideal for resolving smaller construction disputes without the cost of hiring attorneys.

The Simplicity of Small Claims Court

One of the most surprising things about small claims court is how simple the process is.

Cases move quickly.

Hearings are usually brief.

Judges focus primarily on the evidence presented.

This means that the party who is **organized and prepared** often has a major advantage.

Judges appreciate clear explanations.

They appreciate organized documents.

They appreciate timelines that help them understand what happened.

A confused presentation can weaken even a strong case.

A clear and organized presentation can make a powerful impression.

The Timeline Strategy

One of the most effective ways to prepare for small claims court is to create a **clear project timeline.**

Construction projects involve many events over time:

- contract signing
- work performed
- payment requests

- change discussions
- conflicts or disagreements

Without a timeline, these events can feel scattered and confusing.

But when they are organized in chronological order, the story of the project becomes much easier for the judge to understand.

A simple timeline might include entries such as:

January 5 — Contract signed

January 12 — Work begins

January 20 — Additional work requested

February 2 — Payment delay discussed

This type of structure allows the judge to follow the events step by step.

The Project Notebook Method

During one particularly stressful dispute in my own contracting experience, I learned an important lesson about documentation.

Because the project had become increasingly tense, I began keeping a dedicated project notebook.

Each day I recorded:

- the work performed
- conversations that occurred
- requests that were made
- any unusual events on the job site

Over time, this notebook became a powerful record of the project.

But I also began documenting something else that turned out to be surprisingly valuable.

I documented **the pressure of the situation**.

Construction disputes can become emotionally intense.

In my notes I described how the situation felt day by day.

Some days the pressure felt manageable.

Other days the situation felt like being **pursued by a lion** or **squeezed by a boa constrictor**.

These descriptions may sound unusual, but they helped illustrate the level of stress and pressure that developed as the dispute escalated.

When organized properly, notes like these help paint a clearer picture of what was happening during the project.

They show that the dispute did not appear suddenly—it developed over time.

This type of documentation can help a judge understand the human reality of the situation, not just the paperwork.

Organizing Evidence

When preparing for small claims court, both contractors and homeowners should organize their evidence carefully.

Important documents may include:

- the construction contract
- change orders
- invoices and payment records
- photographs of the work
- written communication such as emails and text messages
- project timelines or jobsite notes

These documents should be arranged in a logical order so that the judge can review them quickly.

Clear labels and simple explanations help the court understand the evidence without confusion.

Presenting Your Case

Small claims hearings are usually brief.

In many cases, each party may only have a few minutes to explain their position.

This means your explanation must be clear and focused.

The best approach is often to explain three things:

1. What the agreement was

Explain the contract and what work was expected.

2. What happened during the project

Use your timeline and documentation to describe the events.

3. What resolution you are requesting

Explain the amount of money or outcome you are seeking.

Keeping the explanation simple helps the judge follow the story easily.

Professional Conduct in Court

Even though small claims court is less formal than traditional litigation, professionalism still matters.

Judges pay close attention to behavior and credibility.

The party who appears calm, organized, and respectful often gains an advantage.

Avoid emotional arguments.

Focus on facts.

Let your documentation speak for itself.

A clear and professional presentation demonstrates credibility and responsibility.

The Power of Preparation

Small claims court may seem intimidating at first, but preparation makes the process far easier.

Contractors and homeowners who organize their documents, prepare their timeline, and present their case clearly often achieve better results.

The court is not looking for dramatic arguments.

It is looking for the **most reliable version of the facts**.

When those facts are supported by strong documentation, the path toward resolution becomes much clearer.

The Final Lesson

Construction disputes are never pleasant.

But they can be navigated effectively when contractors and homeowners understand the systems available to resolve them.

Communication, documentation, mediation, and negotiation all play important roles.

Small claims court simply provides one final option when other methods fail.

By understanding these processes, both contractors and homeowners gain the ability to resolve conflicts more intelligently and move forward with confidence.

Chapter 12

The Contractor Protection Framework

A System for Preventing and Resolving Construction Disputes

After years in the construction industry, one lesson becomes clear:

Most disputes are preventable.

Not every conflict can be avoided. Construction projects are complex, and unexpected situations will always arise.

But contractors who operate with the right systems dramatically reduce the number of disputes they face.

Throughout this book, we explored how conflicts develop and how they can be resolved. We examined the role of communication, documentation, mediation, negotiation, and small claims court.

All of these ideas come together in what I call the **Contractor Protection Framework**.

This framework is a simple system that helps contractors protect their businesses, manage disputes professionally, and maintain strong relationships with clients.

The Five Pillars of Contractor Protection

The Contractor Protection Framework consists of five core elements:

Contracts

Payments

Crew

Documentation

Dispute Resolution

When these five areas are managed properly, contractors gain a strong foundation for running a successful construction business.

Let's look at each pillar.

1. Contracts

The contract is the starting point of every project.

A clear contract defines the expectations of both parties before the work begins.

It should outline:

- the scope of work
- payment terms
- timelines
- responsibilities of both parties
- how changes to the project will be handled

Many disputes begin because contracts are vague or incomplete.

Contractors who invest time in clear agreements reduce confusion and prevent misunderstandings later.

A good contract is not just a legal document.

It is a **communication tool** that sets the tone for the entire project.

2. Payments

Payment structure plays a major role in construction disputes.

Contractors must balance two important realities:

They need steady cash flow to operate their business.

Homeowners want assurance that work will be completed properly.

A well-designed payment schedule creates balance between these needs.

Typical structures include:

- deposit payments

- progress payments
- final payment upon completion

When payment expectations are clearly defined, both parties understand the financial structure of the project.

This prevents many conflicts before they begin.

3. Crew

Construction projects rely on teams.

Even small projects often involve subcontractors, assistants, or suppliers.

Managing these relationships effectively is essential.

A contractor's reputation depends not only on their own work, but also on the professionalism of the people working under their supervision.

Strong crew management includes:

- clear expectations
- organized scheduling
- professional conduct on job sites

A well-managed crew helps projects move smoothly and reduces the likelihood of mistakes that could lead to disputes.

4. Documentation

Documentation is one of the most powerful tools a contractor possesses.

Photos, written communication, change orders, and project notes create a record of what occurred during the project.

When disputes arise, documentation replaces memory and speculation with facts.

Contractors who document their projects consistently gain a significant advantage.

Documentation protects the contractor, clarifies the project history, and often resolves disagreements before they escalate.

5. Dispute Resolution

Even the best contractors occasionally encounter conflicts.

The difference between successful contractors and struggling ones often lies in **how disputes are handled**.

Professional contractors approach disputes strategically rather than emotionally.

They understand the stages of the **Construction Dispute Pyramid**:

Communication and documentation

Mediation and negotiation

Litigation

Most disputes should be resolved at the lowest possible level.

Clear communication and professional negotiation often prevent conflicts from escalating into legal battles.

When mediation becomes necessary, preparation and organization help both sides reach practical solutions.

The Professional Advantage

Contractors who follow the Contractor Protection Framework gain several advantages.

They reduce misunderstandings.

They maintain stronger client relationships.

They handle disputes calmly and strategically.

Most importantly, they protect their reputation.

In today's connected world, reputation travels quickly.

Contractors who resolve disputes professionally build trust and credibility within their communities.

That reputation becomes one of the most valuable assets in the construction business.

The Construction Resolution Series

This book is only the first part of a larger system designed to help contractors and homeowners navigate the legal and practical challenges of construction projects.

The books in the **Construction Resolution Series** explore these topics in greater depth.

Construction Mediation: From the Job Site to Resolution

Understanding how disputes develop and how they can be resolved.

The Construction Dispute Playbook

Exploring the legal rules that shape construction projects.

Mechanic's Liens Made Simple

Understanding how contractors secure payment for their work.

The Contractor Survival Guide

Practical strategies for running a successful construction business.

Together, these books provide a comprehensive roadmap for navigating the realities of the construction industry.

Final Thoughts

Construction is one of the most rewarding professions in the world.

Contractors build the homes where families live, grow, and create memories.

But construction also brings challenges.

Projects involve money, expectations, and complex logistics.

Conflicts sometimes arise.

The key is not avoiding conflict entirely.

The key is understanding how to manage it professionally.

When contractors operate with strong systems, clear communication, and careful documentation, most disputes can be resolved efficiently and respectfully.

My hope is that the ideas in this book help contractors and homeowners approach construction projects with greater confidence and clarity.

Because when both sides understand the process, everyone benefits.

Projects run more smoothly.

Disputes are resolved more efficiently.

And the work of building continues.

Reader Assistance Notice

If you have questions or need assistance related to construction disputes, mediation preparation, contractor documentation, or related matters, you may find additional resources through Lexington Legal Solutions.

For information about educational resources, dispute guidance, document preparation assistance, and available services, visit:

Lexington Legal Solutions

www.lexingtonlegalsolutions.com[1]

The resources available through Lexington Legal Solutions are intended to help contractors, subcontractors, and homeowners better understand dispute resolution options and project documentation practices.

1. http://www.lexingtonlegalsolutions.com/

Don't miss out!

Visit the website below and you can sign up to receive emails whenever Nicholas Salerno III publishes a new book. There's no charge and no obligation.

https://books2read.com/r/B-A-KCMK-RJUCJ

BOOKS 2 READ

Connecting independent readers to independent writers.

Did you love *Construction Mediation*? Then you should read *The Battle Plan Against Addiction*[2] by Nicholas Salerno III!

[3]

The Battle Plan Against Addiction

Actively help a friend, family member, or loved one fight the battle of addiction. Understanding the addict and addiction. Your role in all this, and reconnecting back to self. Putting together an intervention and getting them the help they need. Coaching, and further assistance. Lots of resources and links to further education on all topics discussed, and much more.

By Nicholas Salerno III

---

2. https://books2read.com/u/31l7Pa

3. https://books2read.com/u/31l7Pa

Also by Nicholas Salerno III

Contractor Protection
Construction Mediation

Dude Smith
The Adventures of Dude Smith

Lexington Legal Solutions
The Art of U P L

Living Temple
Our Lady and the Living Temple

PULP Comic
Lady On The Road
The Wanderer (comic/manga)

Robot Girl

Robot Girl "Escape to Paradise"

Screenplay

Smoke and Blood

The fantastic dog adventures of Kudo

The Greatest Dog In The World

Superhero Dog And Friends

The Fantastic dog adventures Of Kudo

The Wanderer

The Wanderer, Saving Paradise

Standalone

Pulp Reader

The Origins of Santa Claus

The Battle Plan Against Addiction

The Scroll Of Elijah

Painting Your Beautiful Home

WW3 Isn't What You Thought It Would Be

They Hid The Sky

Bring Down Babylon

Penelope

Don't Give It Away
Lost Equity

About the Author

Nicholas Salerno III is a contractor, dispute resolution specialist, and founder of Lexington Legal Solutions. With more than a decade of experience in residential construction and project management, he has worked on a wide range of projects and encountered many of the real-world disputes that arise between contractors and homeowners.

Through his work in mediation training, construction documentation, and dispute preparation, Salerno focuses on helping contractors and homeowners better understand how construction conflicts develop and how they can be resolved efficiently.

He is the creator of the **Construction Dispute Pyramid**™ and the **Contractor Payment Triangle**™, frameworks designed to help construction professionals navigate disputes and protect their businesses.

Read more at lexingtonlegalsolutions.com.

www.ingramcontent.com/pod-product-compliance
Lightning Source LLC
LaVergne TN
LVHW090426210926
848480LV00002B/700
* 9 7 9 8 2 3 3 8 7 0 9 4 1 *